It's Not Any House You Know

New Myths for a Changing Planet

It's Not Any House You Know
New Myths for a Changing Planet

by Spencer B. Beebe

Artwork by Jacques Flèchemuller
With a Foreword by Wade Davis

For S. and W.

Contents

Foreword

Spencer Beebe has spent a lifetime (well almost—don't count him out just yet) on the outer reaches of conventional thought about people and place. He has built an organization, Ecotrust, that is unmatched in the world in its courageous exploration of the marriage of ecology and economics in ways that are tangible, practical, investment-worthy, and replicable. Spencer has built and been a diligent student among a community of fellow travelers whose thought leadership and willingness to challenge our most cherished orthodoxies are a gift to the world that transcends mere metrics and travels beyond political boundaries.

Spencer's passion for the last quarter of a century has been his home, a place he has come to call Salmon Nation. It is one of the richest bioregions on Earth, and it has been perfect canvas for Spencer's curiosity, matched only by his capacious ambition to express itself in lasting and inspiring ways.

Whether floating an Oregon stream, landing a floatplane on a British Columbia lake, talking to businesspeople in San Francisco, or freezing his butt off in a sub-Arctic bird blind, Spencer is constantly searching for good ideas about how to live well, which means live wisely, on a planet on which wisdom often seems in short supply. He is in some ways a shy person, but he is seldom alone, because his urge to share his home is infectious, and his instinct has always been that by sharing positive experiences of people and place, he will inspire even the best thinkers to think harder, and even the most daring doers to do more. I suspect he is also canny enough to realize that bringing smart, fun, creative people into his world is one way to make his life more interesting—and to make Spencer look smarter than he really is.

Jacques Flèchemuller is a French-born artist, billed as "the master of the incongruous, making serious art with frivolous intent." I didn't know of his work till now, but he has a global following, is represented by Spencer's wife Janie's gallery, PDX CONTEMPORARY ART, so it makes total sense that he would end up in Spencer's orbit and that they would create something whimsical and serious in equal measure, which is what you hold in your hands now.

Spencer has long maintained that the world's ails don't call for more prescriptions. What we need is more celebration—of the ordinary and of the extraordinary. We need new fractals, different dimensions of thought and action, and his particular bias is that the source of much of what there is to learn about how to live well alone, and together, exists in plain sight—on the ground we stand on, the forests and rivers and lakes we have been gifted, the cities we've built, in the genius of living well—and well within our means.

He believes in the power of myth as probably the most fundamental ingredient in shaping new narratives of how to learn from the places that we love, and to afford them the same duty of care we naturally offer our families and friends and colleagues. Fortunately for us, Spencer takes good notes, and some of the wisdom that he has harvested over the decades is now collected here, in a slim volume that can be thought of as a companion to his earlier book, *Cache*. This is more catalyst than book—a short, high-spirited provocation that asks us to expand our thinking beyond conventional politics and polemics, to allow for emergence from unusual channels, in unusual ways.

Spencer and Flèche, as the artist is known, took off for Joseph Creek, in northeastern Oregon, in the fall of 2017 and spent a week fly-fishing for steelhead, talking, thinking, writing, and painting. Their burst of creativity is captured here. This is not a *Sand County Almanac* or a *Walden*, although there is a strain of Leopold and Thoreau—or better yet Audubon (Spencer is an avid birder)—in our man Beebe. Spencer and Flèche made no attempt to match prose and images. They just challenged each other to put down what they know in a way that responded to the country and each other's company. The result is this playful but serious invocation for us all to rise above the obvious, and to imagine anew the very idea of human nature.

It is a rare gift they have given us, to do with what we will.

—Wade Davis

It's Not Any House You Know

The Young Man and the Merlin

A young man trying to grow up. Eighteen and just a week from driving across the country in a hundred-dollar '52 Dodge fluid drive sedan to start college. Time to leave home in the outdoors, a large comforting family, rivers, forests, birds, and a childhood practice of falconry. Time to focus on school, academics, the all-important liberal arts degree.

First, however, he and his parents were staying at a friend's house where he was taking care of a golden eagle on a final trip to the Oregon countryside. He awoke early on a late summer day on the banks of a beautiful river in Central Oregon. That cold morning, he was walking down a river bank of blue bunch wheatgrass, white alder, and pungent sage, flushing California quail and listening to the cackle of orange-and-black Bullock's orioles. As it turned out, it wasn't so much that he was bird-caring or bird-watching as that the birds were watching him.

Suddenly—over a light fog lifting in the morning air and the gurgle and rush of a big, wild river in a deep, cliff-lined canyon—a flash of dark perfection: quick wing beat with primaries just flicking, moving fast upstream.

A kestrel? No, too big, too dark, too strong.

A sharp-shinned hawk or male Cooper's hawk? The flap-flap flat glide of an accipiter, the true hawks of age, smaller versions of the venerable goshawk? No—long, pointed, not rounded, wings. Too fast.

A tiercel prairie falcon? No, too small.

Something new, something different, distinctive, unusual. A merlin perhaps?

Wandering and wondering then in a haze, the young man walked barefoot on warming soil on a narrow trail back to the house and his duties feeding Goldy, the eagle. College, college—pay attention!

Back at the house, the young man's father said, "Look in the Dodge! Bob was standing on the foot of the lawn casting a fly on the morning rise when this small, fast bird flew right into his line, got entangled. He reeled it in, and I put the bird in a cardboard box in the back of the car so you could tell us what it is."

The young man looked. Dumbfounded, he saw a gorgeous, young, male black merlin, the selfsame bird he'd seen flying upstream on his morning walk. A new bird. The rare coastal subspecies of the merlin; relatively large, relatively dark (which is how cold and wet environments tend to differentiate subspecies, like the Peale's falcon; a big, dark, beautiful subspecies of the peregrine that breeds in coastal British Columbia and Alaska).

Here was a whole new species that would teach him one more—no, many more—things about the very distinct nature of a particular subspecies adapted uniquely to the coastal temperate rain forest of North America, to usurping an old crow's nest in a high Sitka spruce above a bog where dragonflies and small birds would provide food for the nestlings at the very right time their feathers were developing in the blood of a casing. Every feather on that bird slightly different than its neighbor, adapted to the function and location on its body, its coloring refined over the millennia to provide both attraction to its mate, camouflage to its prey, and distinction in its surroundings. Every bob of its head, the dark malar stripe below its eye, the fine feathery hairs and the cone in its nostril, adapted to the very particular geography of home.

Well, of course that young falcon went off to college with the young man, accompanied him hooded to freshman-year classes on his left fist, leaving the right hand free to take notes, and they flew on blackbirds and meadowlarks after classes in the fields nearby. "Exeter" was his name, and he taught the young man what it meant to be a merlin. Not a Coopers, or kestrel, or peregrine. A black merlin, one who flies hard and direct on small birds, strikes and carries the prey to a tree or high perch to pluck and eat rather than landing on the ground like most larger falcons taking larger prey.

Exeter distracted the young man from studies, of course. A C-average in his first quarter elicited a harsh letter from his father to put away childish things and get cracking at school, on his career, on becoming a proper and productive young man. But nature had other ideas, and had done its trick. The falcon built a relationship, taught his course, and was later returned to the wild. The young man went on with his life, changed forever.

⋋⋌⋋⋌⋋⋌⋋⋌

Was there something altogether serendipitous or prescient about that rare young falcon finding that young man at that particular moment on a wild river where his father, grandfather, and great-grandfather had camped and fly-fished for one-hundred years? That young man was me, of course. Nature boy. Majors in economics and forest ecology in college and graduate school, a lifetime now in land conservation. And a lifetime bushwhacking the wiggly path towards a deeper synergy between people

"Exeter", drawing by the author

and place. Because it seems the right and the necessary thing to do.

This introductory story of Exeter and me is in part a story about leaving home, but it is also a story about *finding* home, about finding what Scott Russell Sanders calls "a rightness, an at-homeness, a knitting of self and world." No easy task. People sometime ask me if it's hard to train a falcon. I try not to laugh, but the simple truth is that the falcon trains you, not vice-versa. Among the things it trains you in are integrity, purity, beauty, health, instinct, personality, uncluttered vision, freedom, and tenacity. But mostly, a falcon is a model of attentiveness. When you're too close to a situation, step back and rise up. Seen from above, the environment that surrounds you provides a plethora of clues that were there all the time.

Thanks in part to Exeter, my lifetime quest has been to learn to live well as an inseparable part of the larger living community of life. How might I live a good life that maintains, protects, and indeed restores the home, the full migratory home, of the black merlin from Mexico to Alaska? Not as an aside, something extracurricular, but as a central way of being, while earning a living and growing my own family. I seldom knew where I was going, but I knew where I wanted to get to: home. I figured that, as with Exeter, I would learn from nature as I went. And I have—or, more accurately, I am.

I've written in an earlier book called *Cache* about how this quest translated into my founding of the non-profit organization Ecotrust and what that entailed. In the last chapter of that book I cited a passage from Oregon-born writer William Kittredge: "We live in stories. What we *are* is stories. We do things because of what is called character, and our character is formed by the stories we learn to live in." In this small book I want to share ten stories for you to live in. I like to think of them as parables, but in fact they are all true stories: some, like the story of Exeter, are from my own experience and some are ones that friends have shared with me. What the stories have in common is that, like parables, they contain lessons that can be applied to new ways of seeing, of believing, that might help bind the human spirit in a new adventure of discovery.

The stories speak for themselves, but I've added my own commentary without, I hope, becoming overly didactic. If I occasionally slip in what seem to be brags about Ecotrust, you will perhaps forgive my paternal pride. You can read the stories in any order you choose, and you may, of course, find other lessons in the stories as well. That's fine; we're all in this together. That I will become repetitive is inevitable, since the small truths each story contains really come down to one big truth: without the full array of biodiversity and its attendant life-support systems we are alone in the universe. Without Exeter there is no life on Earth.

Finally, along with these stories I've included some paintings by Jacques Flèchemuller. An astute reader—even a not-so-astute reader—might well ask what these humorous drawings have to do with anything. Certainly they are not "illustrations" in the sense that they illustrate the stories. What they do illustrate is the importance of whimsy to counterbalance what at times seems the overwhelming nature of our current ecological, not to mention political, crises. More than ever, perhaps, we need to maintain a sense of fun even as we grapple with issues that are deadly serious. "Deadly Serious Whimsy"—sounds like a good name for a band. We need bands, because we need to dance and sing. We need to celebrate, because surely mere survival is not the best we can do, or the most we should shoot for. We can do without many things in these difficult times, but laughter is not one of them.

Apples and Oranges

A kindergarten class in Wenham, Massachusetts, north of Boston: two five-year-old children, a boy named Tom and a girl named Katie, sit at a table. At the suggestion of their teacher, they are drawing houses—presumably, their own.

Tom begins by drawing a square frame, then a triangular roof, a rectangular chimney, and several windows in front, predictably quartered. He adds some smoke coming out of the chimney and a few flowers in front for color—a house you'd call a house, unqualified.

Katie begins by drawing three sides of a rectangle, using the bottom of the page as the fourth side, and then adds a small circle inside the rectangle on the left-hand side, about half-way up—apparently a door with a doorknob. She then takes a scissors and cuts along the left side and across the top of the rectangle, folding the paper back along the right side and, in effect, opening the door.

Tom, watching, says nothing, but his expression conveys that he already considers the scissors a serious violation of the contract to "draw" a house.

Next, Katie begins making scribbles some distance to the left of the open door. She makes these with a great deal of conviction and without the slightest hesitation, but they are unquestionably scribbles. It is as if, once inside, she knows enough to know that furniture is only one dimension of the real, and not the most engaging as houses go.

"What's THAT?" Tom demands.

Katie pauses, looking not at Tom but at the scribbles. "That's a. . .stairway," she says.

Before Tom has time to protest, Katie begins making a different set of scribbles above the others. These scribbles are angular and jagged, whereas the previous ones had been circular and flowing, but they elicit the same response from Tom: "What's THAT?"

Katie looks at her handiwork. "That's an. . .attic," she says—the same pause, the same satisfaction in her ultimate declaration.

"You're crazy!" Tom says, and he means it. Katie says nothing. Against the grain of Tom's solid house, she goes on drawing: attic, stairway, scribbles—"house." That's what she calls it, but she knows.

Finally, Tom can take it no longer. "That's not the way to draw a house!" he complains loudly.

Katie could well reply, "Failure to believe in ghosts betrays a lack of imagination." But she doesn't; she's five. Instead she says, without so much as stopping or looking up: "It's not any house you know."

The ancient Greek word for house, *oikos* (οἶκος), refers to two related but distinct concepts: the physical house itself and the people who dwell there. Its meaning shifts between one and the other depending on translation and context, which can lead to confusion. I spent a good deal of my early career dealing with organizations that, with the best of intentions, wanted to improve or save the house while not giving due consideration to the people who live there—their ambitions, their strengths and shortcomings, their dreams. In a word, their culture. Who are we to say to such people, "That's not the way to draw a house!"?

Significantly, *oikos* also provides the prefix "eco-" for both "ecology" and "economics." The former has to do with knowledge (-logos) and the latter with management (-nomei). The common root would suggest that ecology and economics are integrally related, as I believe they are. This belief—that conservation and development are flip sides of the same coin—has been at the root of my work to put ecology and economics back together again, to explore the economy of nature and the nature of economies.

That confusion about the meaning of *oikos* is also at the core of the decidedly different ways Katie and Tom envisioned and drew their respective houses. Tom focused exclusively on the literal, physical properties of his house, what he could see and touch. Katie followed suit—for a while. She not only made her door look like a door but cut it along two edges so it could open: she out-Tommed Tom in his ability to be representational.

But once she had opened the door, Katie used a different approach altogether to represent what went on *inside* her house, the felt dynamic among the family that lived there, whereas Tom's house was defined by the physical man-made barriers that separated it from other houses. Katie's stairway and attic bridged the gap between the seen and the

known, as one might greet a living tree as a friendly sibling. Except that Katie's stairway wasn't friendly; her attic—what she called the attic—was downright scary, more scary, in fact, than it was an attic. Either approach, the physical or the felt, is valid enough within its own context; it all depends on where you choose to direct your attention.

And where we choose to direct our attention will be determined in large part by our culture. It comes with the territory, and we learn it early. For example, studies have shown that American parents, introducing toys to their babies, tend to stress learning the names of objects: "That's a car. See the car? It's got nice wheels. See the wheels?" By contrast, parents from Asian cultures, showing their baby the same toy, are more likely to omit the names of the objects altogether and to rehearse social interactions: "Now, give this to me. See? Thank you. Now I give it to you." Such exchanges between parents and their babies convey not just the rules of language, but important parts of the culture. Without being aware of it, the American parents are conveying one of the central tenets of our scientific worldview—that the world, like Tom's house, is essentially a collection of physical objects.

And to the extent that language shapes culture, culture also shapes language—that is, limits those things that we are able to talk about with personal conviction or public credibility. The Haisla people of the Kitlope River Valley in British Columbia express their attitude toward the rest of nature in this way: "We do not own the land; the land owns us." This idea is so foreign to our current worldview as to be almost incomprehensible except in the sentimental way that we often interpret indigenous peoples' concepts. We can pretend to understand it but we seldom, to borrow a phrase, test it against the bone.

When I hear people talk about whether our children will be able to forgive us for what we're doing to nature—destroying biodiversity and so on—

I'm not inclined to disagree. But I want to add that what our children might be least likely to forgive us for is that we have depleted language to the point where they cannot talk about nature except in material terms. Because if they have no language for the internal or felt experience of the natural world that passes as currency in the public forum, then they will be truly lost. They might well feel that they share a common bond with all living things, but they will have no way to make this real to themselves or to *their* children, because we will have left them too few words with which to express it.

What we need, I think, is a new worldview, a kind of informed imagination, that will somehow combine the figurative and the literal, the internal and external. Because these need not exist side by side in separate compartments as they do in our current worldview. That they do exist that way is itself a result of our current scientific mindset, whose great gift is for separating. Renard Strickland in his book *Tonto's Revenge* refers to apple societies and orange societies. A former dean of the University of Oregon Law School and, not incidentally, part Cherokee, Strickland writes, "It is often difficult for these two societies to understand each other because their fundamental approaches to life are opposite ends of the scale of perception." Traditional indigenous societies, he points out, have generally seen the world in a holistic way in which environment, culture, food, security, health are all a part of a larger collective whole, like an apple. Only modern Western industrial societies segment and separate environment, jobs, art, religion, law, and culture, like an orange. This leads to, among other things, the preposterous notion that one must choose between jobs and the environment.

As with Katie's and Tom's houses, how we view and interact with nature will depend on whether we direct our attention to its physical properties or to the relationship between the living creatures, including ourselves, who dwell there. Ideally, as I suggested above, we can do both, but we are a long way from attaining that ideal. In fact, we have focused our collective attention for so long on the physical aspects of the natural world—nature as useful commodity—that to attempt to talk about the felt aspects of nature is to invite the accusation, in this counting house of a world, that "You're crazy." Which means, in effect, "If you can't count it, it doesn't count; if it isn't matter, it doesn't matter." To which a person more in tune with the family of all living things can only reply, a bit sadly, "It's not any house you know."

More Than Just Trees

A poet and a scientist are sharing a breakfast of trout on the porch of a one-room cabin on remote Clayoquot Lake in British Columbia. They are the only two humans at the lake, well out of earshot of the protests about logging rights that are going on in Tofino, twenty minutes away by float plane. Above them, lofty red cedars, western hemlocks, Pacific silver and Douglas fir, and Sitka spruce form an almost unbroken canopy. It would be hard to imagine a more beautiful place, teeming with the power of wild nature.

The scientist is a young man just out of college who manages this research station for the Clayoquot Biosphere Project. He spends much of his time at this cabin, which he helped build from cedar logs that he also helped mill. His job now is to gather and record data about the lake—wildlife activity, changes in water surface temperature, aquatic insect hatches, and so on. The poet is a guest, flown in from Portland to get the lay of the land to better understand and write about this place and its history.

Both men are fishermen—after a fashion. The scientist fishes with a Zebco rod-and-reel combo that he bought for fifteen bucks Canadian from the Co-op in Tofino. The poet has brought his own tackle and has introduced the scientist to an Italian-made lure, the Panther Martin, a red-and-yellow spinner with which he managed to catch two thirteen-inch cutthroat trout when he went along with the scientist on his morning canoe tour of the lake. On returning to the cabin, the scientist dutifully records in his log book: "June 28, 1993: The fish here seem to like Italian food."

As the two enjoy their breakfast, the scientist is talking about why he does what he does. "The science we do here doesn't amount to much. The whole idea of having a cabin here is to establish a research presence and keep the timber companies out. I don't have any objection to cutting down trees," he goes on. "I built my house in Tofino out of wood." He looks up at the trees and pauses, weighing what he is about to say, then goes on: "But you can't live out here for weeks at a time without knowing that these trees are more than just trees. There's a presence here. And the thing is, after I've been out here for awhile—well, I'm afraid to go home again."

This was a remarkable thing for the scientist to say. It was an observation totally foreign to his training—one that didn't allow for the kind of empirical evidence he'd been sent to collect—and both men were aware of this. The poet opened his mouth to say something, then realized that what the scientist was talking about was a mystery—a word that derives from the Greek verb muo (μύω), which literally means to close your mouth. The poet closed his mouth.

✕✕✕✕✕✕✕

When it comes to learning from nature, trees are among our greatest teachers—until, that is, we turn them into pulpits. Trees teach by the example of their integrity, by being what they are supposed to be. We learn from being around them in the same way that we profit from the presence of human beings who exhibit this kind of integrity, though these, I'm afraid, are unfortunately much harder to find. It follows—and I believe it is true—that to the extent that we are not doing what we should be doing, trees will make us aware of this, which may not always be pleasant. In any case, they are among our best examples of what we can be, and the more we are in their presence, the more likely we are to imitate that example.

This, I think, was something of what was behind the young scientist's observation that these trees were "more than just trees." By an accident of extended proximity, combined with a particular kind of attention, he sensed that these trees were like him in a way that mattered. Many of us have had this experience when confronted with awesome power of wilderness; it is like coming into a room you think is unoccupied and suddenly becoming aware that someone you don't know is sitting there. As the essayist Gary Snyder has written, "An ancient forest is more than a stand of timber: it is a palace of organisms, a heaven for many beings, a temple where life deeply investigates the puzzle of itself." Or as the young scientist observed, "There's a presence here." He sensed, and gradually learned, that these trees could tell him something about how to live his life, and that he could, if he chose, come back and check himself against their knowledge, the way we check whether a table we are building is true by reading the small bubble on a level.

I single out trees, but what I'm saying about trees can also be true of animals. Woodrow Wilson once observed, "If a dog will not come to you after having looked you in the face, you should go home and examine your conscience." But animals are more capable of imitating and being influenced by us to the point where they become not so much models as mirrors—and, in the case of some pets, not always of our best selves. Trees never do this. They are necessarily influenced by our treatment of them, but unlike both animals and humans, they never respond in kind to meanness or imitate their oppressors. It was, I think, the prospect of losing touch with these ancient, silent teachers that made the young scientist "afraid to go home again."

A wise man once told me that the most important right is the right to be responsible—and trees, left to their own devices, will be "responsible." From a human perspective, they are responsible for shade, cool, and oxygen, to mention just a few. In the presence of water and sunlight, trees take in CO_2 through the stomata on the underside of their needles (or leaves), capture the C (carbon) into carbohydrates (wood), and respire the O_2 (oxygen). Photosynthesis. That's good news for creatures who like to breathe. The process is a miracle. It's complicated but simple really. We'd be wise to help it along.

I would also argue that part of the responsibility of trees is to be a resource for economic development, in the same way that springboks, say, are responsible for being a food source for lions. But when the fulfillment of this kind of responsibility interferes with the primary responsibility of any species—namely, to survive—then a line has been crossed that must be reversed. There is a growing recognition, not just among environmentalists but among the general public, that we have crossed that line in our relationship with the rest of the natural world. It is this recognition, much more than any legislation or technological expertise, that must and will be the prime mover of the transformative change that we so sorely need if we truly want to "go home again"—and to not be afraid.

Look, A Gift Horse

Erskine Wood was thirteen years old when his father sent him to spend time with Chief Joseph of the Nez Perce Indians of Wallowa country. The famous Nez Perce chief was living on the miserable scrap of land in central Washington to which he was allowed to return after the long war—after the sad and pathetic defeat at the Battle of Bear Paw, just short of the Canadian border—and his internment in Oklahoma.

Young Erskine's father had been General Howard's aide-de-camp in that war and is said to be the one who wrote down Joseph's words at the final battle of defeat at Bear Paw, Montana, "From where the sun now stands, I will fight no more forever." He had thought the whole long pursuit of Joseph and his people a travesty of justice, and later went on to become the chief's close friend. Later still he would become a successful lawyer in Portland, a poet, painter, and bohemian Renaissance man who fought for women's suffrage as well as proper treatment of Native Americans.

During Erskine's second autumn with Joseph, his father insisted that he ask Joseph if there was anything he needed. After a season of wearing moccasins, living in a tepee, hunting with Chief Joseph, and working with a young Indian boy to take care of the horses, Erskine asked Chief Joseph if there was anything

he could do for him. Joseph thought and at last said, yes: "We have no good horses. We are horse people and have bred and run with thousands of beautiful Appaloosa horses for centuries in wide winding valleys. Yes, I would love to have a good stallion to upbreed our pony herd."

Erskine later recalled that this request was "Just the kind of thing in his Indian life that he needed, and of course well within the ability of my father to get for him." But at age fourteen, young Erskine assumed that his father would want to give Chief Joseph something like the return of his Oregon homelands and would not consider a horse an adequate gift. And so he never told his father what Joseph had asked for. But the older he got, the sadder he grew about what he would later call his "utter stupidity." He died in 1983, at the age of 103, still haunted by his failure to fulfill Chief Joseph's request.

In 1997, Erskine's grandchildren, knowing that this was the major regret of their grandfather's life, decided that late was better than never. They sought the most beautiful Appaloosa horse they could find, a stallion whose owner at first said no, she couldn't possibly sell her horse. When she learned of the story, however, she relented. And the family tracked down the nearest living descendant chief of the non-treaty Joseph's band of the Nez Perce. A great ceremony was held in the Wallowa foothills, speeches were made, a gorgeous black-and-white stallion appeared and went to a new home among Joseph's nearest descendants. After 104 years, Erskine's obligation to his old friend was at long last fulfilled—better late than never.

☆☆☆☆☆☆☆

On my mother's side of my family there is history with Civil War casualties, West Point graduates, and Seventh Cavalry Indian fighters, one of whom was Charles Erskine Scott Wood, young Erskine's father. I knew "Young Erskine" only as "Woody," and grew up on his lap urging him to tell more stories about the proud and peaceful leader named Joseph. In truth I have always been a wannabe Nez Perce Indian. I suppose that says a lot.

Despite the fact that Chief Joseph didn't get his horse, ultimately the story has a beautiful ending, one that helped salve the consciences of many. That gorgeous horse died twenty years after he was given as a gift to Chief Joseph's descendants. I don't really know the rest of the story. Perhaps he lived well in a beautiful pasture in the high Yakima Valley and was ridden happily across native grasslands, pine forests, and along stream bottoms under a cottonwood gallery forest. Perhaps not.

But the story is a reminder that in Indian country, a gift represents a relationship, a give-and-take that acknowledges participation in and dependence upon the very specific boundaries, culture, and abundance that constitute "home." A gift-giver becomes more powerful in the ceremonial festival known as "potlatch." The receiver then lives with the obligation to respond in kind. In a gift-exchange economy, every gift imposes obligations—to protect it, to use it well, to pass it on. Lewis Hyde, in his book *The Gift*, puts it this way: "The only essential is this: the gift must always move. There are other forms of property that stand still, that mark a boundary or resist momentum, but the gift keeps moving."

A gift is not forgotten. It lives on as a symbol of a reciprocal relationship. Hence the first salmon ceremony in so many coastal tribes was one in which gifts received from the Salmon People came with the knowledge that their source— that place, that river, that rich run of fish—must be cared for, nourished, and prayed to like the god it was. When we establish such a relationship with nature, we respond to it as if to fellow beings, not as strangers or owners or even stewards. We realize that to destroy nature's renewable wealth is to destroy ourselves as surely as anything can. A gift-exchange economy includes a built-in check against such destruction.

What Woody realized was that he had missed an opportunity—indeed, ignored an obligation—to participate in this relationship of gift exchange. What his descendants realized is that it is never too late to do so. This latter realization should give us heart in a time when, all too often, we are inclined to think that it may indeed be too late to change our relationship with the rest of nature in ways that matter enough.

What might a gift-exchange economy look like in the 21st century? Actually, we need look no further than the drawings of Jacques Flèchemuller that accompany these stories. Like any artist, Flèche knows that part of his work can't be made, it must be received. And having accepted what has been given, either in the terms of inspiration or of talent, the artist feels compelled to pass it on to an audience. A gift-exchange economy is as simple and complex as that, and as powerful: *the gift must stay in motion.*

But you cannot reciprocate a gift if you don't know where it comes from. It is significant that the human race evolved first in small groups around particular habitats, learning the particular habits of prey and predator alike, as well as where to find water, shelter, and food. Similarly, gift exchange starts locally and expands outward—family, friends, neighbors, community, and so on—but has its natural boundaries most clearly defined by vested interests and shared cultural values. Why locally? Because local people cannot afford to see their environment as an object to be exploited. Their economic well-being, and indeed their social well-being, is interwoven with the environment in such a way that either developing or caring for their environment means developing or caring for themselves in that environment. Local people don't want to "save" the environment any more than they want to exploit it; what they want to do is live in it. If they are to do this, they must concern themselves with conserving and restoring the resources of the very specific place on which their lives and livelihoods depend.

Can we apply the principles of gift exchange to other kinds of commerce than that of the Native American potlatch or the artist's imagination? Of course we can. Through careful stewardship and harvesting, local communities can export ecosystem goods and services and use some of the revenues to maintain the productivity of their ecosystem gift exchange on a grand scale. On the national and global scale, certainly, the demand for such goods and services—high quality timber, organic farm products, fish and shellfish, wild areas for tourism—is increasing even as the supply dwindles. Those who can fill this demand—not to mention the public and their growing demand for clean air and unpolluted water—will enjoy an increasing advantage in the marketplace. Moreover, the current expansion in socially responsible investing may well give ecologically sound businesses greater access to capital, off-setting the competitive edge of exploitive businesses. And just as the economy of gift exchange can provide a working example for modern rural communities, such communities can, by embracing similar values, provide a working example of ecologically sound business practices in a market economy.

I'm not saying that any of this will be easy, but I say it's not too late to try.

Jane the Giant-Slayer

As a small girl, Jane had no intention of growing up to be a giant-slayer. Giant-slayers, generally speaking, do not hail from Scranton, Pennsylvania. They do not have first names like Jane and last names like Butzner. They do not have their first job as an unpaid assistant to the women's page editor at The Scranton Tribune.

The Jane of this story did not have access to any weapons designed to slay giants. Unlike David, she didn't even have a slingshot. What she did have were an active imagination and a boundless curiosity about what worked and what didn't—and why. She was a keen observer and no slave to convention. The poet William Meredith has written, "The worst that can be said of any of us is: he did not pay attention." That was Jane's weapon—she knew how to pay attention. In spades. And it paid off. In spades.

Jane began her unlikely career as a giant-slayer in 1956 at a conference on urban planning at the Harvard Graduate School of Design. She was forty at the time, a magazine writer and mother of three who, truth be told, was attending the conference only by accident. The person who had been invited to speak couldn't attend and sent Jane in his place—this despite the fact that Jane had written only one major article about urban planning. Jane's speech wasn't a long one—only ten minutes, in fact—but in those few moments she told the gathered experts on modern city planning what they least expected to hear—that their work as city designers contributed to a social poverty worse than any slums.

Wham!

Needless to say, many of the giants present were not impressed at being summarily cut down to size by this upstart woman with no credentials in their field. But one of them, The New Yorker's *renowned architecture critic, Lewis Mumford, had the critical acumen to observe that Jane's Harvard talk had "established her as a person to be reckoned with. . . a new kind of 'expert'":*

> *This able woman had used her eyes and, even more admirably, her heart to assay the human result of large-scale housing and she was saying, in effect, that these toplofty barracks that now crowd the city's skyline and overshadow its street were not fit for human habitation.*

In the years ahead, Jane's "upstart" ideas—thanks in large part to who she was and the books she wrote—would come to be seen as mere common sense. The moral? Pay attention, speak your mind, and who knows? You might just slay a giant.

⋇ ⋇ ⋇ ⋇ ⋇ ⋇ ⋇

If you haven't guessed it by now, the woman in the story is Jane Jacobs, *née* Butzner, the celebrated author of numerous books but best known for *The Death and Life of Great American Cities,* which the *New York Times* has hailed as one of the ten most important books of the last century.

Jane Jacobs was, and will always be, one of my heroes. I first met her when she was in her 70s and toward the end of her long and extraordinary career. I invited her to join Ecotrust's board, which, remarkably, she did. I also invited her to accompany us on a float trip down the Middle Fork of the Salmon River in Idaho, and she accepted despite not being in the best of health at the time. A city girl at heart and never an enthusiastic outdoorswoman, Jane was a great sport and enjoyed the trip immensely.

In *The Death and Life of Great American Cities*, Jane had spoken of diversity, density, connectedness, reciprocity, and constant adaptation—an organic process that starts at a very fine granular level on the sidewalk or workshop or street corner and grows, bottom up. She saw what she called "differentiation emerging out of generality," the constant process of people inventing a new good or service to the changing needs and wants of consumers. She saw "import substitution," the critical economic expansion process of people making something locally that was previously imported from somewhere else. She saw the bartender on a busy New York street watching out for school kids playing on the sidewalk. She saw all this and she wrote, in words no longer than two syllables, "We expect too much of new buildings, and too little of ourselves."

Later in life, Jane Jacobs turned her fierce powers of observation to consider ecological processes, evolution and bio-mimicry in nature. There she saw the same processes at work that she had seen in economic development: one species differentiating into subspecies, then two species as they exploited a new niche, creating new networks or communities of species, storing yet more energy and creating more opportunities for further differentiation and expansion.

She began working on a new book called *The Nature of Economies*. I will never forget the day she told me that she saw Ecotrust doing precisely what she was writing about. We had introduced Willapa Bay oysterman and fishermen to higher-end, differentiated markets for high-quality, small, fresh oysters on the half-shell, and beautiful fresh chrome Chinook salmon sold directly to Portland markets rather than to the commodity fish buyers at the dock. She saw our efforts to restore the diversity of species and age-classes of the forest as further differentiations aimed at growing and selling more western red cedar, as well as western hemlock, Douglas fir, and Sitka spruce—more eggs in the basket of changing market conditions. I like to think I knew this, but it was humbling to hear it from Jane Jacobs.

What Jane observed was that effective economic development is actually one and same process as evolutionary or ecological development. And why not? Because we humans are all part of the larger community of life, of nature. Surely the great achievements of our species—art, symbolic language, garage-door openers, the Global Positioning System—are as much natural wonders as a beaver's dam or a robin's nest. We marvel, as indeed we should, that certain moths have learned to communicate over as much as two miles of thick woods by releasing subtle chemicals that prospective mates can detect at levels measured in parts per million; we find it less—or less *natural*—of a marvel that we can pick up a cell phone and hear accurate copies of sounds vocalized a split second earlier by a counterpart on the other side of the world. Surely there is something near-sighted in our tendency to exclude whatever is human from the sum of biodiversity, as if sonatas and spaceships did not represent positive contributions to biotic richness, or qualify as examples of this planet's special, natural genius.

This was the final theme of that great, inquisitive observer: "Human beings exist wholly within nature as part of the natural order in every respect." She saw this as the basis of what she called "a more reliable prosperity." Not, it should be noted, "a reliable prosperity"; she was too street-smart to assume that such a condition can endure in a changing world. But, yes, a "*more* reliable prosperity." Jane Jacobs died on April 25, 2006 at the age of 89.

In the immortal words of Yogi Berra: "You can observe a lot just by looking."

Pachico and the Whale

In the 1850s, Charles Melville Scammon, a Maine-born whaling captain (later turned naturalist) sailed south from San Francisco and discovered the fabled nursing grounds of California gray whales in the warm lagoons of the Pacific coast of the Baja peninsula. Long the source of myth among the New England whalers, the nursing grounds were a place where bulls, cows, and calves were found in unimaginable numbers in shallow waters following a 5,000-mile migration from the Bering and Chukchi Seas.

On making his discovery, Scammon took 47 whales yielding 1,700 barrels of oil worth $15,000, a small fortune for the time. He returned only a few years later to find the secret place a noisy camp of hundreds of whalers from all parts of the world, a sea turned red with the blood of horrific industry. Some of the whalers would target the calves with their harpoons to lure the protective mothers to their deaths. In a rage some cows would attack the whale boats and earned the reputation as "the devil's fish" for their ability to destroy them with a slash of their giant flukes. The lagoons were soon hunted to exhaustion.

For a hundred years gray whales were killed across the Pacific, driving the western Pacific population to near extinction, and by the 1940s just a few thousand survived in the eastern Pacific, following an historic pattern in

which Atlantic populations of gray whales had been exterminated by the mid-1700s.

As remarkable, and depressing, as this history is, the story of the whales' recovery is even more astonishing. It began in 1972 when a fisherman from San Ignacio Lagoon named Francisco "Pachico" Mayoral was approached by a forty-ton, almost fifty-foot-long gray whale while fishing with a friend in a small "panga," a boat less than half the length of the whale. Fishermen had been warned from childhood to keep their distance from the feared devil's fish with their long history of conflict with whalers. The whale approached so close that Pachico was able to reach out and touch her gently on the head, his heart pounding, not sure what might be the whale's next move. After almost forty minutes of playful curiosity, she gently slipped away. Pachico returned to his village to tell his friends about the whale's approach and behavior, only to be met by derision and disbelief. Everyone in the village knew of the dangers of the devil's fish and her destructive nature. No sensible person dared approach a whale. It was clearly not part of the local culture, the mythology of that place.

But Pachico was sure the whale had chosen him to re-establish an ancient connection. Gradually over the ensuing years, friendly whales, particularly cows with their new-born calves, approached other fishermen and visitors, and from that a whole whale-watching industry has emerged, attracting as many as five thousand tourists and school children annually. All this has helped to rebuild a local economy, increasing opportunities and the diversity of revenues to local people.

Today it's quiet and peaceful in the whale-watching camp on the south side of San Ignacio, this sixty-square-mile lagoon on the central west coast of Baja California del Sur, Mexico. Half the world's wintering population of black brant, terns, loons, grebes, and miscellaneous shorebirds of every description fill the air; bottle-nosed dolphin play in the surf; four of the world's seven species of sea turtles are found in its waters. Most importantly, the gray whales thrive, dozens of them rolling in an outgoing tide.

⋊⋉⋊⋉⋊⋉⋊⋉⋊⋉⋊⋉⋊⋉

Silas Beebe—my great, great, great grandfather and namesake to my eldest son—was a whaling captain out of Mystic, Connecticut, not unlike Charles Scammon. Silas filled his mid-1850s ships' logs with tales of slaughter of whales and elephant seals from both the North and South Atlantic. On the back of his portrait that hangs over our living-room fireplace is a postcard describing a successful load of spices and trade goods from the Caribbean, along with a clandestine hold of opium—just in case. Some family skeletons survive just fine outside of closets.

The story of Pachico and the whale is an extraordinary tale of wild nature reconnecting with local inhabitants, and rebuilding an economy based on the intimate and inseparable connection between people and place, between the human species and the larger community of life of which it is part. It is about as good an example of an organic model of development as one might imagine. The fishers of San Ignacio Lagoon now have two sources of potential revenue instead of just one—a more reliable prosperity.

The people of San Ignacio Lagoon believe that community-based development which emerges naturally and incrementally from the intimate relationships that have evolved over the millennia in that very particular and distinctive place is a better, more resilient, more reliably prosperous approach than large-scale, top-down initiatives that spend more money, destroy both the environment and the distinctive culture of traditional livelihoods, provide only temporary benefits to outside people and businesses, and are often transitory in nature. The whales of San Ignacio Lagoon suggest that this is true.

But this is just a small part of an emerging global story. The burgeoning whale-watching business of San Ignacio Lagoon coincided with a global environmental campaign to prevent a large international industrial company from turning the whole area into a gigantic salt factory, one that might degrade both the fishery and the whale population, leaving local people with fewer rather than more options, and less local control. The campaign was successful. Across the Baja Peninsula and the entire Sea of Cortés, fishermen, scientists, conservationists, and Mexican state and federal agencies and institutions are now working together to improve the well-being of both the environment and its residents. Man and the Biosphere reserves and marine protected areas are maintained in large part by the people who live there.

But the story is also an example, on a small scale, of what we need to do on a much larger scale. By changing their perception of the whales, the people of San Ignacio Lagoon changed their behavior, and then their economy, and, ultimately, their whole way of life. Not by committee or top-down decree, but through one-by-one acceptance of a new way to see these creatures with whom they shared a common history and a common place. Just as the villagers changed their mythology about their relationship with the whales, we need to change the mythology by which we view the rest of nature.

By mythology here I mean a collection of stories by which people give meaning to their lives. We all create personal myths about ourselves, of course; someone once observed that the French author Victor Hugo's biggest problem was that he thought he was Victor Hugo. But the kind of myths I have in mind are not created by a single person; they emerge out of the fears and aspirations of a people living in a particular place over a long period of time. They are not arrived at by consensus, nor are they imposed like commandments or company or government policies. They emerge out of and shape cultural values slowly, much as the ocean shapes a rocky coastline or a river cuts through narrow canyons and wide valleys, defining itself as it goes, and then redefining itself over and over again.

Our myths—our collective beliefs—are the product of stories that we tell one another over time until those stories become part of a larger narrative, a people's collective psyche. Why stories? Because, unlike lectures or proclamations or legislation, stories don't tell us what to do. Instead, they provide examples of what we *can* do. They spark our imaginations and set us to thinking. They prompt us to ask questions like "What if. . . ?" and "What about this?" Not just any stories, however. Stories only carry conviction and prompt us to act when they speak truth to our experience, and to the values those experiences impart.

The dominant mythology by which much of the Western world views nature dates back to the 17th century, when the English philosopher Francis Bacon sounded the battle cry of a "New Science" based on "the power and dominion of the human race over the universe." Bacon proclaimed: "We must put nature to the rack, and compel her to answer our questions." It was a remarkable, and remarkably male, metaphor—a kind of prototype of sexual harassment—and one that would become more prophetic as the new science begat new technologies, which in turn begat industrial development. Well, nature's been on the rack for more than three hundred years now and she's answered some important questions that have greatly benefitted humankind. But, as might be expected from Bacon's metaphor, she isn't holding up all that well.

As far as what a new mythology might look like, that remains to be seen. But the story of Pachico and the whale stands as a kind of talisman of hope that we are capable, at least, of moving in the right direction. It's a start.

Dumb Ideas

On December 10, 1967, a twin-engine Beachcraft H18 airplane took off from Cleveland, Ohio, destined for Madison, Wisconsin. The passengers included, besides the pilot, seven members of a band called the Bar-Kays, which had just finished the first leg of a cross-country tour. The pilot had been warned of bad weather and advised to postpone the trip, but the band members voted not to disappoint their fans in Madison. The pilot had a mechanic check the plane, then took off. Four miles from Truax Field in Madison, the pilot radioed for permission to land. Shortly thereafter the plane stalled, then crashed into Lake Monona, killing seven of the eight people aboard, including the pilot.

One of those killed was the bandleader, a young singer/songwriter who was in the middle of an unfinished recording session at Stax Studio in Memphis at the time of his death. The album he was recording just days before his death contained a new song in a style that was atypical for him, more brooding than the kind of romantic style he was known for. People told him this was a dumb idea. The Stax studio crew were opposed to including the new sound, some going so far as to say that it would damage the label's reputation. Even the singer's wife didn't care for the melody. Worse, in place of the vocal fade-out rap that was earmarked for the ending, the singer substituted whistling, leading one of the engineers to comment, "You're not going to make it as a

whistler." The singer's collaborator and back-up guitarist for the Stax house band complained that the lyrics were off in one place, but the singer was sure the song was going to be a hit and replied, "That's the way I want it." The last words he said to the collaborator were "I'll see you on Monday." That Sunday the plane he was in crashed; the singer was dead at the age of 26.

The new song was released a month later. The singer had been right; it was a hit. It reached number one on the Billboard Hot 100, the first posthumous number-one single in U.S. chart history, and stayed there for two months. It sold approximately four million copies worldwide and received more than eight million airplays. The song ranked as the sixth-most-played composition on American radio and television in the 20th century. Rolling Stone named it No. 26 on its 500 Greatest Songs of All Time. Today, 50 years later to the month, it remains a song that you might be likely to increase the volume for when you hear the opening line: "Sittin' in the morning sun. . . ."

The song, of course, was "The Dock of the Bay"; the young singer/songwriter was Otis Redding.

⚹ ⚹ ⚹ ⚹ ⚹ ⚹ ⚹

At the time of his death, Otis Redding was bent on reinventing himself. His inspiration, like that of many musicians in 1967, was the Beatles' *Sgt. Pepper's Lonely Hearts Club Band* album. Not so much the music itself as the expanded sense of what was possible: *If they can do that, what might I do?* In art, as in life, the biggest influences have less to do with content or style than with courage. Redding had the courage to trust his instincts when everyone told him he was making a mistake. As a result, he wrote and recorded a song that has lived twice as long as he did and is still going.

Why do important ideas, in retrospect, always seem to be the ones that people tried to talk you out of? Skeptics, naysayers, doubters: *Start an environmental bank? What a fool! You know nothing about banks* (true) *and banks know nothing about the environment* (less true now than it used to be). To which I might reply: *OK—now that we've settled that, let's get started.* And at Ecotrust, we did, helping to start an environmental bank that has grown to $1 billion in assets.

Of course, some dumb ideas turn out to be—well, really dumb. Some things work, others don't. Many good ideas are buried in existing but often overlooked places. But I've come to think that if I have an idea that everyone thinks is great, it's probably not worth doing. Why bother? Someone else must already be doing it. And if what we're already doing is so great, why are we confronted with global climate change and the erosion of planetary life-support systems? If this were third grade, we'd be sent back to second grade. *Hey, humans, you flunk!*

If you follow the international conversation about climate change at all, you may well have come across the term "anthropocene." It's a description that scientists have in recent years used to define the geological epoch in which we now live. The term, literally meaning "The Age of Humans," refers to the fact that people are now a primary influence on the key systems that maintain the conditions for life on the planet, and that ozone depletion and global warming are products of that influence. Not many of us think in terms of geological epochs, but if we did, it would be hard to deny that the scientists are right—though not so hard that many people insist on doing so. Some critics argue, with pure hubris, that the term is more political than scientific, a bull-horn wake-up call to join the effort to reduce greenhouse gasses and escalate dependency on renewable energy sources. Others embrace the concept zealously as yet another tool in their doomsday rhetoric, focusing on the question of whether we can survive the anthropocene and answering with a resounding "No!"

For those of us who still believe in science, it's hard not to accept that the anthropocene is real and a very big deal. Messing with planetary life-support systems is a fool's errand of unimaginable proportions. But I'm optimistic enough to believe that we have the collective technological know-how to ultimately reverse global warming and restore planetary life-support systems to something like their full function. Technological know-how is what we're good at, and many organizations, including my own, are hard at work on finding solutions to the urgent issues that climate change confronts us with.

The notions at the heart of this book, however, have more to do with imagination than science. Even if technology saves us from reaching the brink (or, more likely, helps us claw our way back after we've passed it), what then? Will we have learned anything about ourselves? Will our cultural values have changed? Will we do anything differently? Will we be any closer to living well, being happy, and taking care of this, our only home?

There are people—smart people—who see that we can solve problems such as global warming with what we currently know. Paul Hawken's inspirational project Drawdown explicitly states that a "qualified and diverse group of researchers from around the world" has "uncovered a path forward that can roll back global warming within thirty years. It shows that humanity has the means at hand. Nothing new needs to be invented. The solutions are in place and in action."

Those are heartening words; and pursuing regenerative forestry, farming, green building, reducing food waste, and the many other solutions in Drawdown are indeed the very specific things we can and must do. We do indeed have the technological know-how required to reduce carbon emissions sufficiently to roll back global warming. But will this outcome in itself help change our mindset, the way we see the world, in a way that leads to a new mythology of people and planet? To paraphrase Einstein,

it's an illusion to think that we can solve problems without changing the mindset that created them.

To do that we do need something new, something we don't already have, something that, in fact, we have yet to imagine. The Drawdown manifesto goes on to say, "We chose the name Drawdown because if we do not name the goal, we are unlikely to achieve it." One might counter that if we *do* name the goal, we run the risk of achieving only that. And if we achieve only the goal we can identify before we start, then we might as well be on the dock of the bay, whistling and "wastin' time." As the song has it, "Look like nothing's gonna change / Everything remains the same." It may indeed *look* like that at times, but in fact the reverse is true: nothing remains the same; *everything's* gonna change. The tools we need to adapt to inevitable but unforeseen changes are not so much a panel of experts, but imagination and flexibility. Like the song says, "I can't do what ten people tell me to do."

I don't mean to suggest that in addressing our current environmental crises we need imagination to the exclusion of technology or vice versa; we need both. We need technology and accurate data to, as Hawken says, "arrive at viable solutions and accelerate the knowledge of what is possible." But we also need imagination to approach problems in unforeseen ways, to develop new ways of valuing natural systems, parts, and places of the world and change the very boundaries of what is possible. What we need are grand experiments in institutional resilience in what Joshua Ramo has called "The Age of the Unthinkable."

But mostly, I think, we need individuals who, like Otis Redding in 1967, aren't afraid to start out, trusting themselves and their urge to create something different and of value. I'm heartened to see that young people today, who generally prefer to think of themselves as "social innovators" rather than "environmentalists," seem to know this. They seem to know that fear and urgency, however justified, are not the soil from which wise decisions are likely to spring, and that playfulness and having fun are also important.

I'm thinking of people like Erin Shrode and "Project Green," which invites young adults to compete in fun, high-impact daily challenges that touch on various green categories like transportation, fashion, and food. "The first year," Erin says, "we had no idea if people would stick with it and keep doing these kooky things." I'm thinking of people like Jessie Housty and the Heiltsuk First Nation's Koeye Camp, which integrates science and cultural rediscovery into a fun and challenging education program for kids. "I hope I can always remain nimble, because there's no one path," Jessie says. "But the seeds are there, and I look forward to spending my life helping them grow."

Community catalysts like Erin and Jessie know that creating anything of lasting value requires first, patience, and second, flexibility: helping local communities develop their capacity to move in directions that make economic and ecological sense means that everyone involved must be ready for surprises and be willing to change course when the situation calls for it. They know that the process can be long, slow, evolutionary, trial-and-error, adaptive, and experimental, but always with social benefit. They understand the importance of learning by going. No one ever learned to ride a bike by thinking about it.

Much of what I have been saying has been said better by Ralph Waldo Emerson in his essay called "Self-Reliance." I can think of no better baton to hand off to the young people on whom, inevitably, the future of this planet depends:

> There is a time in every person's education when you arrive at the conviction that envy is ignorance; that imitation is suicide; that

you must take yourself for better or worse as your portion; that though the wide universe is full of good, no kernel of nourishing corn can come to you except through your toil bestowed on that plot of ground that is given you to till. The power that resides in you is new in nature, and no one but you knows what it is that you can do, nor do you know until you have tried. . . . Trust yourself.

The Magic Canoe

At age ten, a boy named Cecil Paul was removed from his Haisla native village of Mis'kusa on the banks of the Kitlope River in north-central British Columbia. He was taken in his moccasins by the Royal Canadian Mounted Police to a residential school in Port Alberni on Vancouver Island, a victim, like thousands of young native children, of Canadian government policies designed to convert native people into proper Christian white children. Generations later, the Chief Justice of the Supreme Court of Canada would refer to these policies as amounting to "cultural genocide," and no-one disagreed. The government, abetted by the Church, had sought, in the words of Canada's first Prime Minister, Sir John A. Macdonald, to "take the Indian out of the child."

In the case of Cecil Paul, it didn't work.

Cecil suffered greatly at the Port Alberni school. Hundreds of miles from his home, forbidden to speak the only language he knew, beaten, sexually assaulted, and then discarded by the school at age fourteen, his spirit broken, not knowing how to get home. He washed up on Skid Row in Vancouver, depressed and habitually drunk. He eventually went north, at one point snagging a job in a fish cannery called Butedale, where he fell in love with a young white woman and she became pregnant. He proposed marriage, the only decent thing to do. Instead he lost his job after the cannery manager, the girl's father, declared: "No way is my daughter marrying a fuckin' Indian." The child, a girl, was given up for adoption. Cecil headed to the fishing town of Prince Rupert and, once again, drowned his sorrows in drink.

But after a time a voice beckoned, an ancestor. It was his grandmother, calling him back to Kitamaat Village, where the survivors of his people, the Henaksiala people, had amalgamated with the Haisla First Nation. She bade him return to the Kitlope River, to Mis'kusa—to go all the way home.

But home was vanishing before his eyes. The Haisla and Henaksiala traditional territory of some four-million acres of marine fjordland, islands, mountain streams, huge Douglas fir, Sitka spruce, and cedar were almost all now part of a "tree farm license" that was being rapidly logged, while commercial fishing fleets were depleting rich supplies of crab, shrimp, halibut, and salmon. What Cecil called his "bank" was being drawn down by the same forces of colonialism and industrialization that took him from his homeland as a child. The social effects on Kitamaat Village and the Haisla community were taking a deadly toll on youth and adults alike in alcohol, drugs, and suicide. Cecil wondered aloud if there would even be a Haisla people in the future: "Who are we in this strange modern world?"

Then, on a salmon fishing trip to the Kitlope River, something unusual happened to Cecil and his companions. As Cecil tells it, four young white people "fell out of the sky." In point of fact, a de Havilland Beaver float plane landed, unloaded four people and their gear, and departed.

Around a campfire that night the "Boston people" and the villagers talked. For three more days they talked and fished together and shared stories. These whites had learned that the Kitlope River was the largest pristine coastal temperate rain forest watershed anywhere in the world. No roads, no logging, no dams, no hatcheries. All eight hundred thousand acres from mountain top at eight-thousand feet, high glaciers, waterfalls, magnificent forest, all the way to the estuary where fresh water met salt, and nourished large flocks of migrating waterfowl, shorebirds, and returning salmon and steelhead of all six species. It was about to be logged, and Cecil and his companions were talking about what to do. He wasn't even sure he could convince his own villagers to fight for their land.

Then and there, Cecil and his companions decided to team up with the Boston people. Over the next four years they would work together to characterize their home and share their stories with growing numbers of scientists, journalists, and environmentalists. They just kept falling out of the sky, these people, and together they paddled the territory and explored their many options in what Cecil came to call a supernatural or "magic canoe": the more people that came, the bigger the canoe grew.

This expanding polyglot of strangers paddled to unknown horizons, to the provincial capitol in Victoria, to Ottawa, to office towers in Vancouver, to make their case to government officials and the forest products company that held the rights to log and feed their sawmill in the north. The Haisla and Henaksiala ventured as far as Stockholm to visit a folk museum where they found Cecil's brother Dan's totem pole, which had stood at Mis'kusa at the mouth of the Kitlope River before being sawn down and taken to Europe without Dan's permission by a Swedish consul of an earlier age.

Back in British Columbia, they made their case to arrest the planned logging to the minister of environment and took him to the Kitlope—climbed mountain slopes, ate salmon, floated rivers, built campfire—and at every turn, shared their stories.

There was another surprise while paddling that magic canoe. It turned out the minister of the environment, a minister of "the Crown" as they are known in colonial parlance, had a surprising story of his own. Before becoming a politician and eventually a cabinet minister, the environment minister had been an Anglican Church minister in a coastal Indian village near Prince Rupert. He had adopted a daughter and named her Cecilia. She grew up with the minister's family and friends, one of whom was a Haisla woman whom Cecilia called "aunt Louise." Unbeknownst to her, Louise was Cecil's sister, and Cecilia was Cecil's daughter.

That's a whole lot of magic right there, but there's more. The forest company voluntarily gave up its right to log. The Kitlope was protected; it would not be and it has not been logged. The stolen totem pole was repatriated from Sweden to Henaksiala territory—and in the spirit of gift exchange, a new pole was carved in Kitamaat and sent to Sweden in its place. And then one day, Cecil, and Cecilia, and the minister, went back to the Kitlope together.

Today, government maps list the place as the Kitlope Heritage Conservancy. "You guys call it the Kitlope," Cecil once said. "But in our language we call it 'Huchsduwachsdu Nuyem Jees.' That means the land of milky blue waters and the sacred stories contained in this place. You think it's a victory because we saved the land. But what we really saved is our heritage, our stories, which are embedded in this place and which couldn't survive without it, and which contain all our wisdom for living."

〜〜〜〜〜〜〜

What moves me most about this story is not that I was privileged to be one of the first passengers in Cecil's magic canoe, but the courage that he and the villagers displayed in trusting white men, against all odds, to do the right thing. Most people, in my experience, are understandably wary of outsiders, especially those who claim to have their interests at heart. Outsiders' interests and those of the local communities may often be similar but not identical, and various interests within a community will routinely be at odds with one another. Hence, an important part of building a "magic canoe" is to help ensure that all concerned parties are directly involved in setting the course, planning the means, and sharing the accountability and the benefits. This will vary depending on local cultures, traditions, politics, and circumstances, but it invariably involves negotiation. In the case of protecting the Kitlope I learned far more from Cecil and the Haisla than they did from me. And what I learned from them, they in turn had learned from the specific place in which they live. More gifts, being passed along.

What is remarkable about Cecil's story is that this great helmsman, so to speak, was about as far removed from the conventional sources of power as could possibly be imagined. And yet he demonstrated that he and people like him have the power to transform not only their own lives but the lives of their communities. For that is exactly what Cecil did: he invited Boston people into his canoe, and they paddled together to a place that contains, in his words, "all our wisdom for living." We can all learn by traveling to unexpected places, together, with faith in the human spirit—even in spirits that seem broken from the outside—that new possibilities might emerge. What is thrilling is to find on-the-ground examples of alternative ways of being and living in the world, ways that might never occur to us on our own.

Preserving the Kitlope is just one such example, an important early victory in what became a region-wide campaign that led, in time, to a celebrated conservation and development initiative called the Great Bear Rainforest. Like the Haisla, the Heiltsuk and neighboring First Nations that occupy the central coast of British Columbia, and, farther west, the islands of Haida Gwaii, had been fending off rapacious logging of their traditional territories for decades. Despite their protests, one small tract of some 250 acres was acquired and clear-cut, then sold for the development of a sport fishing lodge. When the tract and lodge came on the market, however,

Howard and Devon Buffett and Peter and Jennifer Buffett donated a million dollars to Ecotrust and we worked with Ecotrust Canada to convey fee title to the Heiltsuk. The altogether unsuitable lodge was later burned to the ground, the remnant logging equipment removed, and the site has gradually been rebuilt using Heiltsuk-milled wood and featuring their art and craft. Solar panels, a new micro-hydro facility, vegetable gardens, a cafe, and cabins for staff and guests have evolved without a master plan—organically, bottom-up—with culturally appropriate materials. Logging companies have donated cedar. Carpenters and craftsmen who stumble into the Koeye by sail have volunteered labor and love. Donors and supporters and well-meaning journalists, rather than being solicited, have volunteered their support.

It is no stretch at all to see that what the Heiltsuk have built in Koeye is yet another magic canoe. The Heiltsuk have an expression in their language, *ṃṇukvs ẃúwax̌di,* which translates as "one mind, one heart." That is, in essence, what propels Cecil Paul's magic canoe, just as many paddlers also helped build a new container for stories in the Koeye. It is not all that different from Jane Jacob's observation about reciprocity and adaptation—an organic process that, in the case of the Kitlope, was launched around a campfire on the Kitlope River and began a journey of adventure.

And the gift keeps moving: we are all paddlers in the magic canoe.

Stop and Smell the Ashes

On September 2, 2017 at 4 p.m. a fire was reported in the Columbia River Gorge National Scenic Area near the town of Cascade Locks, Oregon. The fire grew to 3,000 acres that first night. During the night of September 4th and 5th, east winds, combined with excessive heat, caused the fire to rapidly increase in size, pushing westward. By the morning of September 5th, the fire had grown to more than twenty thousand acres and had crossed the Columbia River into Washington near Archer Mountain. The combination of firefighters, cooler temperatures, and higher humidity helped slow fire growth in the days that followed, but the fire grew to the east and reached almost fifty thousand acres.

By mid-September, six hundred fire personnel were still fighting the flames, people were still evacuated from their homes, Interstate 84 was still closed, and many trails were damaged. On September 19 the National Weather Service and Eagle Creek Fire officials declared the Eagle Creek Fire to be forty-six percent contained, up from thirty-two percent the previous morning. Rain had greatly dampened the fire, allowing three hundred fire personnel to go home, but only after the fire had scorched more than seventy-five square miles and racked up a firefighting bill of at least $20 million. That didn't include things like $2 million to $3 million in lost business in the Cascade

Locks, where evacuations hit at the height of the late-summer tourist season.

A chart of the basic information about the fire includes the cryptic entry: "Cause: human." The human in this case was a fifteen-year-old boy accused of starting the wildfire by tossing fireworks along the Eagle Creek trail. The boy was from a large, church-going Ukrainian family in Vancouver, Washington that was mortified by what happened. He was charged with reckless burning and other offenses in Hood River Juvenile Court. His mother told The Oregonian *that "this is a trauma for him" and "it was his mistake." She said she feared a public backlash and that the boy's school-age siblings might face retaliation. The mother's fear was justified. Public criticism and vitriol followed quickly as news of the fire's cause spread. One person tweeted: "To teen who allegedly started Eagle Creek fire: I hope you land in jail and bankrupt your family over your idiocy."*

Eagle Creek is but one of hundreds of wildfires that have burned in recent fire seasons across the continental West. In response to this latest string of extreme natural disasters, Nature might be justified in saying: "To species that allegedly caused global warming: I hope you and your kind burn in hell over your idiocy."

Happily, Nature doesn't use Twitter.

✕✕✕✕✕✕✕

My maternal great grandfather, Henry Jonathan Biddle, moved west from Philadelphia in 1883, settling on the banks of the Columbia River, just east and north of Portland. A pass on Oregon's Mt. Jefferson and a remote peak in the Rocky Mountains of British Columbia carry his name. He invested in silver mining in Idaho and rock quarries in Washington. Apparently, Henry Jonathan knew something about rock. And in 1905 he found one of particular interest—Beacon Rock, the basaltic remains of a 57,000 year old volcano. Referred to as "Pilot Rock" by Lewis and Clark, it has a commanding view of the very heart of the Columbia River Gorge, the single place where a river cuts east to west through the Cascade Mountains, now a national scenic area.

Having an appetite for adventure and good work, Henry decided to spend three tedious years building a trail to the top of Beacon Rock and later his descendants offered to donate it to Washington as a state park. When the governor of Washington demurred, they offered it to Oregon's governor. But when word got out that this offer just might be accepted, Washington's governor capitulated in favor of the original proposal. Thousands of people every year now scale Beacon Rock to take in the view—including, in 2017, a spectacular view of the fire at Eagle Creek.

All of this family mythology, whether fact or fiction, has led to my particularly romantic attachment to the Columbia River Gorge, its spectacular old growth Douglas fir, high waterfalls, and mountain views. So when the Columbia Gorge fire broke out in the summer of 2017 it threatened not just a place I know, but a place I love. The forests of home were on fire.

Unfortunately, record-breaking fire seasons are becoming all too common. In 2017, over one million acres burned in British Columbia—the worst fire season on record for the province, until even more fire burned in 2018. And more than a million acres more burned in the American interior West. From central Idaho and Montana, to eastern Washington, across Oregon, down through Klamath Country in Northern California, all the way to Burbank—homes, communities, and beloved landscapes are under threat from increasingly devastating fire. Despite the heroic efforts of thousands of firefighters—volunteers, national guardsmen, prison inmate crews, and agency veterans alike—many new fires will burn largely unabated as yet another "hottest year on record" supplants the last.

I've seen many such fires firsthand from the pilot's seat of a small plane. In an admittedly ironic and complicit contribution to this tragic state of affairs, I've flown from Oregon to Alaska to coastal B.C. to the American Rockies and back visiting many remote communities that have called these places home for 10,000 to 15,000 years. My own family has made Portland home for five generations now and we, like so many others around us, have been stunned and saddened to see so much of this place we love go up in smoke.

Meanwhile, 2017's hurricane season back East was one of the deadliest and costliest season on record. Multiple Category 5 and 4 storms made landfall, including three major hurricanes—Harvey, Irma, and Maria—that wreaked unprecedented damage on coastal and island communities. These three consecutive storms claimed hundreds of lives, hundreds of thousands of homes, and over $280 billion in damages. Of course it is necessary to make the usual disclaimer, which is that none of these extreme weather events can be directly and exclusively linked to global warming per se. But these are precisely the kinds of extremes that scientists have predicted will occur as average global temperatures rise as a result of increased greenhouse gas emissions.

If it's not clear what happens when greenhouse gases accumulate in Earth's fragile atmosphere, park your car in an asphalt parking lot on a hot summer day and roll up the windows. Would you leave your kids inside, or your dog? Same general idea. Or consider this: according to the Union of Concerned Scientists, the sea surface temperature in the Gulf of Mexico was between 2.7 and 7.2 degrees Fahrenheit above normal, which allowed Harvey to quickly jump from a tropical storm to a Category 4 hurricane. Houston has now experienced three "five-hundred-year" floods in three years, and the overall number of extreme weather events has risen by forty percent in the last decade as our planet gets hotter every year.

Whether or not one accepts the overwhelming scientific consensus that these extreme climate events are driven largely by the effects of human activity on planetary life-support systems, it's abundantly clear that we need to confront a new climate reality. This alone should convince us that it's high time for a new worldview. Prince Charles, in his book Harmony: *A New Way of Looking at the World,* stated it well:

> When people talk of things like an "environmental crisis" or a "financial crisis" what they are actually describing are the consequences of a much deeper problem…a "crisis of perception." It is the way we see the world that is ultimately at fault. If we simply concentrate on fixing the outward problems without paying attention to this central, inner problem, then the deeper problem remains, and we will carry on casting around in the wilderness for the right path without a proper sense of where we took the wrong turn.

We've been living with a "wrong turn" of epic consequences, our whole model of development turning on the idea that nature—and indeed, other people—are commodities that can be controlled. The careless and casual disregard with which the Eagle Creek Fire began is not only the story of naive and misguided youth growing up in a world disconnected from laws of nature, but also indicative of a more profound naiveté and hubris that the Industrial Revolution and the exploitive mythology by which we live was built on. We can't in fact take life on Earth as we know it for granted. Our individual and collective behavior has consequences.

The quote from Prince Charles reminds me of the old saying that in England things are serious but not desperate while in Ireland things are desperate but not serious. Which in turn reminds me of the American tourist in Ireland who said to an Irish woman, "It doesn't occur to most Americans to be embarrassed that we can speak only one language," to which the Irish woman replied, in a delightful brogue, "Don't you mind—we're embarrassed for ya." Well, folks, make no mistake: the climate crisis is serious and desperate, and it's high time for us Americans to be at least as embarrassed about dragging our feet as other countries are embarrassed for us.

So what to do? What we need to wake up to now is the opportunity for change. Of course the fires and storms produced immediate human tragedies and emergencies of life and property that must be addressed first and foremost. But I would also suggest that it is time to embrace ways of living and doing business that will reduce the effects of climate extremes and honor the interconnectedness of people and place. Because large-scale social change will happen only where people share common concerns, goals, and core values.

But doom and gloom won't get us there, nor will breast-beating. What we need to do instead is to unleash the most important growing resource available to us and to communities worldwide: the boundless imagination of the human mind.

Swimming Upstream

The eggs of a Pacific salmon lie in gravel through the winter as the embryos within develop. In early spring, alevins hatch. These tiny fish carry a food supply—a sac of egg yolk—attached to their bellies. They won't leave the protection of the gravel until the yolk is used up, twelve weeks or more. At that time, the small alevin emerges from the clear, clean gravel in cold well-oxygenated water. The young salmon, now called fry, swim up to the surface, gulp air to fill their swim bladders, and begin to feed.

Sound easy? Think again. The barely one-inch fry (hence "small fry") competes with all the other familial fry in a small pool for limited micro-aquatic insects, avoiding kingfishers, mergansers, and larger predatory fish. After a year or two or three in that small pool, some mysterious genetic signal says to a now five-inch smolt, "Time to head downstream"—and off it goes, traveling at night to avoid unknown predators, swimming miles and miles and miles downstream through new territories before discovering eel grass beds of the estuary. "Watch out for big fish, fishing terns, cormorants, more fish ducks!"

Then, at last, a huge metabolic shift from fresh water to salt water, into the vast ocean itself: seals, even more abundant predatory fish, new sources of food, and one, two, three, four, or even five years depending on the salmon species and particular life history, feeding in the wide Pacific, avoiding the sea birds now, the pods of killer whales, the fishing boats. And then the return home past more coastal fishing boats, sport fishermen on every bank, dams, irrigation ditches ... upstream all the way.

The salmon must return from the ocean to its natal stream to spawn in the gravels of its birth. This journey may be a few miles, from forested freshet near the coast and just a year spent in nearby coastal waters, or it might be hundreds of miles from an interior mountain stream to the estuary, then the ocean, thousands of miles across the Pacific, to coastal Japan, the Sea of Okhotsk in the Russian Far East, the Bering Sea of Alaska; then southbound again, back to that same coastal river mouth, back up the river, up rapids, up one tributary, then another, then another, each the correct turn following the chemical signals of the water back home. Find a mate, fend off competitors, spawn and die so the waters are fertilized by your rotting body, marine nutrients and all, to nourish the next generation.

Maybe one or two percent of fry return as adults, miraculously, swimming against powerful currents to spawn. Only the strong survive, reproduce, and adapt to the very particular nature of every specific part of the ocean and the stream; each reach, each tributary, produces a distinct genetic life history adapted over the eons to those many specific challenges. The chrome ocean adult with light underbelly, most perfectly adapted as camouflage against predators from below; the spotted, dappled blues and blacks and silvers topside, most expertly adapted to protection from above; the power of muscle and fin, the genetic, magnetic memory of every leg of the journey.

At last, upstream, clear clean gravel in cold well-oxygenated water in which to build a redd—a depression created by the upstroke of the female salmon's body and tail. Not just one redd but several, depositing a few hundred eggs in each during the one or two days she is spawning fertilized by the milt of competing males. The eggs lie in gravel through the winter, and the cycle begins again.

Whew!

⚡ ⚡ ⚡ ⚡ ⚡ ⚡ ⚡

Damn (and dam), that's a lot of work! And you thought your life was hard! Upstream all the way and analogous all the way, perhaps, to your daily struggle to accomplish your dreams, to live well, to survive. Is this similar to the great business analyst Peter Drucker's observation that "All grand visions deteriorate into daily drudgery"? When you want to quit, you have to keep going; quitting is not an option.

The story of the salmon is an example of how nature self-organizes in distinctive bioregions everywhere with long histories of human co-evolution. If you have trouble getting your head around the notion of a "bioregion," consider this: Ask Red Sox fans where they're from and they might well say that they are citizens—not of Boston, or Massachusetts, or even New England—but of "Red Sox Nation." And they're proud of it. They choose to identify themselves not by artificial boundaries but by a terrain of consciousness and people supportive of one another around a beloved icon—the Boston Red Sox. Translate that sense of place and belonging into one that is defined not by an iconic sports team but by a place's natural boundaries—its unique combination of plants, animals, geology, climate, water and all the things that distinguish it from other places—and you've got yourself a bioregion.

Where I'm from, we call our bioregion Salmon Nation—the big coastal watersheds of the Sacramento, Klamath, Columbia, Fraser, Skeena, Taku, Copper, and Yukon Rivers and the temperate rain forests from the redwoods of California to the cedar and hemlock forests of southeast

Alaska and adjacent Pacific Ocean. And why not? Is there a more natural north-south relationship between those living in Ketchican, AK; Prince Rupert, or Kitamaat, or Bella Bella, or Vancouver, B.C., and those living in Seattle, Astoria, Portland, even San Francisco—a relationship that encourages greater collaboration than with those living in Calgary or Salt Lake City?

Those of us who live here are citizens of Salmon Nation as surely as we are citizens of British Columbia, Canada, Hood River County, Oregon, or the U.S.A. This is merely an expansive expression of our sense of place, of our "home," growing up where there are lofty Douglas fir, the sweet smell of fresh mint along the rivers, an empty beach in a pounding surf in winter, the call of a raven, the song of winter wrens in the forest under oyster skies, good morning coffee, and a short bicycle ride to work in a walkable city like Portland. All we might ask of fellow-citizens of Salmon Nation is whether they love where they live and, if so, how they might imagine leaving this place a little better than they found it.

Perhaps even more importantly, the diversity, abundance, and resilience of wild Pacific salmon constitute an iconic "canary in the mineshaft," one simple measure of the well-being of both people and place. For if the salmon are not well, then other things aren't right: the ocean's productivity, the clarity and coolness of our rivers, the sensibility of our measures of a reasonable harvest, hatchery practices, or the proximity of grazing and farming near the rivers banks. We can measure other things of course; GDP, employment rates, farm sales, real estate prices, interest rates, or the balance between immigration and emigration can also indicate a region's well-being. But in this part of the world for thousands and thousands of years, the return of salmon has been the singular most anticipated and celebrated event of the year. Perhaps, today, wi-fi speed or a trip to the mall or the results of a Super Bowl get more attention, but what good are they for measuring the health of an economy, the stability of society, the happiness of its people?

The range of Pacific salmon in both its marine and terrestrial components totals some five percent of the Earth's surface. Multiply Salmon Nation times twenty and we have all the world's places and peoples, within which all sorts of nature states or nature nations already exist: the grasslands of the Midwest, "Buffalo Nation"; the temperate deciduous forests and adjacent coastline of the Gulf of Maine, "Lobster Nation." Measures must of course be taken of a region's social and economic as well as ecological conditions. But most importantly, social symbols speak to the sensibilities of people and are broadly embraced when they invoke a sense of place that make sense to people who know it best—its stories, its rituals, its accepted behaviors.

So the question is this: are the geo-political boundaries of nation states—an altogether artificial concept of self-organization—the best way to address the systematic degradation of planetary life-support systems and to govern human relations with each other and with the environment? In today's globalized economy, capital goes where it wishes with little or no regard for geographical or political "nationhood." In the end what matters is whether our region has an environment—in particular, a climate—that supports the diversity and productivity of its human population as well as the full diversity of its ecological parts and processes. Otherwise it is floods, droughts, fires, and the complete inability of our political and governance systems to cope, as appears to be the case both here and around much of the world today.

"Nature nation" or "nature state" is different from, often diametrically opposed to, but potentially synergistic with "nation state" as a political construct. Perhaps it wasn't coincidental that the publication of Adam Smith's *Wealth of Nations* and the signing of the U.S. Declaration of Independence both occurred in 1776. The nation state has ever since,

both here in the U.S. and in most places around the world, been assumed to be the creator of, holder of, and embodiment of wealth.

Except that this idea is either no longer true or should be discarded as largely irrelevant. Nativist attitudes, capital controls, trade policies, tariffs, and such can impede capital flows, but only to a point. Money will go to cities and regions around the world where it finds competitive advantages: labor costs, natural resources, quality of life, local regulatory conditions, and so forth. These are qualities of bioregions, nature states, more than nation states. And regions will increasingly compete based on the distinctive characteristics of place around the world. To create economic opportunity we need to think nature state as much as, or more than, nation state.

So imagine this: what if we helped shape a new myth: the concept of a "nature nation" or "nature state" instead of a "nation state." It's not a complicated idea—simply put, it means building new kinds of communities and identities around natural boundaries rather than political ones. It is not a new idea either, except for people who come out of an industrial-technological heritage. Maps of language and tribal groups around the world describe distinctive communities, tribes associated with distinctive environments. Only in the last few hundred years have we drawn hard straight lines of politics, war, and colonialism.

Also, imagine what might be the natural competitive advantage of nature nations, both to create economic opportunity for more people and to restore the diversity and health of ecosystems and ecological processes. Why not ditch the artificial geo-political boundaries of province and state and nation, and replace them with natural boundaries? Why not build new kinds of identities, some of which will of course turn out to be very old, around those natural boundaries— and *then* feed them back into the political system to create the infrastructure that makes these newly valued ways of living in the world possible?

In effect, the term "nature nation" is just another way of expressing the idea of a "bioregion," a naturally occurring, relatively coherent, landscape-scale geographic area defined by shared ecological characteristics of climate, soil, water, and plant and animal species. Bioregions also generally include shared large-scale human, cultural, and economic characteristics. So really we're simply talking about both people and place—on a scale that matters. We're talking about home.

Because in the end, that's what these stories have all been about—using our imaginations to redefine what we mean by home and, in the process, advance our search for a more reliable prosperity. Going forward, we must organize around and learn from Nature, because we are part and parcel of it. Let's create a new myth of people and planet around a holistic worldview, and grow a movement to improve social, economic, and environmental well-being motivated by hopeful stories about the place, and the places, we call home.

Easy? No way. Upstream all the way? Absolutely. Where do we go to even learn how to start? *The eggs of the Pacific salmon lie in gravel through the winter as the embryos within develop. In early spring, alevins hatch and—* well, you get the idea: it's hard work. It's hard work being a salmon, and it's hard work doing our collective bit to ensure that salmon can keep on being salmon. But it's worth it. Listen and learn and nourish reciprocal, mutually reinforcing relationships. New ideas, 180 degrees to convention. The best ideas are revolutionary in theory but co-evolutionary in practice. It takes a long time, but not forever. Draw inspiration from what surrounds you, and most of all, celebrate possibilities in the unlikeliest of places. Be serious, but have fun.

Acknowledgments

Slight as this volume is, it reflects almost fifty years of trying to knit ecology and economy, people and place, back together again. So there is a small universe of generous and spirited friends, family, and colleagues to thank for experiences shared and lessons learned. A list of them all would be longer than these stories, so many of them will remain un-named but should know that their contributions are deeply appreciated.

First, I want to acknowledge and thank Jacques Flèchemuller for his remarkable skill, infectious love of fly fishing, and generous spirit. Flèche didn't purposely set out to send humanity over a waterfall (front cover) and restate the obvious about who is really in charge (back cover), but such was the result of this short paddle together.

Without my poet friend and Ecotrust's self-styled "nag-in-residence" Gary Miranda you would not be holding this book in your hands. Gary struggled for over a year to wed poetry and inspiration with science and observation, a marriage that at times felt altogether irreconcilable but that we can only hope will stand the test of time.

Ian Gill called on his long career in journalism, as well as his being the only person to have been president of all three Ecotrusts, including Canada and Australia, to selflessly help edit this book towards a more coherent and readable form. Thanks for this and all your other services, Ian.

Thanks too to Wade Davis for his inspiration over the years and for his kind foreword. Wade's twenty-five or so books (I've lost count) put my authorial output to shame, and I can only hope that this present effort of mine lives up to his more-than-generous words.

My cousin Mardi Wood helped square my recollection of her grandfather Erskine Wood with reality in the gift horse story.

The board and leadership of Ecotrust have been remarkably supportive and tolerant of my many aberrations. They share what we call a high tolerance for ambiguity and, time and again, have been willing to jump in the magic canoe and head downstream, and often up, with or with out either map or clarity about what we might find together.

Closer to home, and therefore most importantly, I want to thank my dear companion and wife of more than fifty years, Janie; our four parents who always supported whatever our passions unleashed; and our three wonderful children, Silas, Sam, and Lydia. Janie created the now twenty-three-year-old PDX CONTEMPORARY ART out of sheer will power to do the right thing for the artists she thought she could help, Flèche among them. Sam in particular has been paddling the magic canoe with me as a colleague at Ecotrust for fifteen years and understands as well as anyone what we are all about. He is a skilled scout, diplomat, and ambassador, particularly in Indian country, where he has garnered a deep empathy and understanding.

Finally, my sincere thanks to Gerald Amos, Bill Barks, Jeremy Barnicle, Christopher Brookfield, John Cashore, Sarah Cline, Bobbie Conner, Derek and Sophie Craighead, Gun Denhart, Chris Desser, Lindsay Eberts, Bill Egan, Exequiel Ezcurra, Bob Friedman, Nancy Frisch, John Fullerton, Ron Grzywinski, Kate Warren Hall, Pete and Vanessa Hartigan, Paul Hawken, Carolyn Holland, Jessie and Larry Housty, Dan Kemmis, Hank Ketchum, Jock Kimberley, John Kitzhaber, Jim Lichatowich, Elise Lufkin, Ken Margolis, Francisco and Ranulfo Mayoral, Tom McGuane, Antone Minthorn, Dave Morine, Nell Newman, Jim Norton, George Patterson and Josie Osborne, Cecil Paul, Alana Probst, Ted Ragsdale, Tom Saunders, Nancy Schaub, Stephanie Schlect, Wendy Seldon, Claude Singer, Ofelia Svart, Kat Taylor, Bob Walsh, Dan Wieden, and Katherine Wiley, all of whom contributed their support, thoughts and encouragement to various drafts over the past year of rumination.

Rest assured that this journey is not over. There are more chapters to be written and more stories to be shared, and there will always be more to do. I, for one, can't wait.

About the Author and the Artist

Spencer Biddle Beebe grew up in Oregon fly fishing, camping, and practicing falconry. He has a lifetime commitment to wilderness and conservation and has devoted his professional career to building organizational capacity and exploring new strategies for conservation. He has played a key role in the creation and development of over thirty organizations and programs from Alaska to Bolivia, including helping to pioneer innovative approaches such as debt-for-nature swaps in developing tropical rain forest countries and environmental banking in the Pacific Northwest.

After serving as president of The Nature Conservancy International and founding President of Conservation International, Spencer returned to Oregon and founded Ecotrust, where, over the last 28 years, he has created a new paradigm not only for conservation, but for how we organize our societies and economies around nature. He has pushed Ecotrust to catalyze "practical, radical change" in the way people bank, manage forests, eat, and exercise their citizenship in communities and landscapes from California to Alaska. He currently serves as a board member and founder of Ecotrust, and a founding partner of the Salmon Nation Trust. He is the author of *Cache: Creating Natural Economies* (2010) with his son, Samuel M. Beebe.

Paul Hawken says of Spencer Beebe: "His accomplishments in stitching this wounded world back together are vast, original and matched by a breadth of vision that instills greatness in others."

Jacques Flèchemuller lives and works both in Brooklyn, New York, and in Ardeche, France. As a boy, he first became aware of art through the monthly comic calendars that were given out by the local post office. When it was made evident to him that these images were, in fact, not art, he was devastated. Humor came to be and remains a very important factor in his work.

While he studied drawing in Paris as a young teen, Flèchemuller never considered making a living as an artist. He worked multiple odd jobs, including a stint as a magician in a small circus, a gagman in a dance company, and as a chef on a barge/restaurant in Paris. He is now a full-time artist represented by PDX CONTEMPORARY ART in Portland and shows his work internationally.

Of the works included in this book, he says: "When I think that the piece I'm working on is finished, I call my wife in to look at it. If her response is: 'What an interesting piece!' I dump the work in the garbage bin. If she laughs, then I keep it. (I only work to make my wife laugh!) Up on the mountain with Spencer when I made these paintings, I hoped that the fantastic nature around us would laugh as well. It did. I was very happy."

Wade Davis is an Explorer-in-Residence at the National Geographic Society, named by them as one of the Explorers for the Millennium. Davis holds degrees in anthropology and biology and received his Ph.D. in ethnobotany, all from Harvard University. A writer, photographer, and filmmaker, he is perhaps best known for his book *The Serpent and the Rainbow,* an international best seller later released by Universal as a motion picture.

Davis has been described as "a rare combination of scientist, scholar, poet, and passionate defender of all of life's diversity."